P9-CPV-231

Americans All biographies are inspiring life stories about people of all races, creeds, and nationalities who have uniquely contributed to the American way of life. Highlights from each person's story develop his contributions in his special field — whether they be in the arts, industry, human rights, education, science and medicine, or sports.

Specific abilities, character, and accomplishments are emphasized. Often despite great odds, these famous people have attained success in their fields through the good use of ability, determination, and hard work. These fast-moving stories of real people will show the way to better understanding of the ingredients necessary for personal success.

Father
Flanagan

FOUNDER OF BOYS TOWN

by Charles P. Graves

illustrated by William Hutchinson

GARRARD PUBLISHING COMPANY
CHAMPAIGN · ILLINOIS

Jb
F 583 g
C. 1

For my godchild Mary Stalter Radsch

Acknowledgment:

Father Flanagan of Boys Town, written by Fulton and Will Oursler and published by Doubleday and Company, Inc., was a primary source for much of the material in this book.

Picture credits:

Father Flanagan's Boys' Home, Boys Town, Nebraska: pp. 28, 46 (bottom), 61, 81 (all), 92

Walter S. Craig Film Productions, Omaha, Nebraska: p. 46 (top)

Copyright © 1972 by Charles P. Graves

All rights reserved. Manufactured in the U.S.A.

Standard Book Number: 8116–4571–1

Library of Congress Catalog Card Number: 70–173448

CHICAGO HEIGHTS PUBLIC LIBRARY

Contents

1. Ireland 7
2. America 17
3. A Priest at Last! 23
4. Homeless Men 31
5. Homeless Boys 41
6. "He Ain't Heavy, Father . . ." . . 53
7. The Barefoot Slayer 63
8. Happy Ending to a Sad Story . . 70
9. Boys Town, U.S.A. 79
10. Father Flanagan's Work
    Goes On 89
    Index 95

1. Ireland

When Eddie Flanagan was six years old, his father said, "Son, you're big enough now to take the sheep to the pasture by yourself. Would you like to try it today?"

"Oh, yes!" Eddie cried. He was proud that his father trusted him and was determined to do a good job.

The Flanagans lived on a big farm in Ireland where Eddie had been born in 1886. Though he was thin and not too strong, Eddie had a great deal of energy and ambition.

He took the sheep to a meadow and sat under a tree while they ate the grass. Suddenly, he heard a lamb bleating in pain. Looking about, Eddie saw that a tiny lamb had wandered away from the flock and was caught in a brier patch. Eddie ran to the briers and tried to free the trapped lamb.

The thorns tore at his hands, and they started bleeding, but Eddie went right on working until the lamb was free. Then he lifted it to his shoulders and carried it home.

"Oh, Eddie!" his mother cried. "Your poor hands!" She helped her son remove the thorns while his father treated the lamb.

"You are a good shepherd, Eddie," his father said. "You put the lamb's safety before your own."

"Eddie is always kind and thoughtful," his mother remarked. "He's a big help to me around the house."

Eddie had seven sisters and three brothers, and the children had a lot of fun together playing games, fishing, and swimming in a river near their home. Nearly every night one of Eddie's older sisters, Nellie, played the piano while his big brother, Patrick, accompanied her on

his accordion. Eddie and the other children stood around the piano and sang.

Before going to bed the children always prayed with their mother and father. The Flanagans were devout Catholics and attended church in Ballymoe, a nearby town.

One morning Eddie went to mass alone with his mother. As they were leaving the church, Father Featherstone, the priest, stopped them.

"Good morning, Mrs. Flanagan," he said. "You have so many children I can't keep them all straight." Pointing to Eddie he asked, "Which one is this?"

"Well, his full name is Edward Joseph Flanagan," his mother said, "but we call him Eddie."

Shaking hands with the boy, Father Featherstone asked, "What are you going to be when you grow up?"

"I don't know," Eddie replied.

"I think I do," Father Featherstone said. "I believe you're going to be a priest."

Eddie's blue eyes flashed with pride. He knew that Patrick was planning to be a priest. Eddie thought he would like to be one too.

On the way home Mrs. Flanagan said, "I know you would make a fine priest,

Eddie. You love to help people, and you are such a good student."

Eddie had always liked to read and often took books with him to the meadow when he tended the sheep. His brother Patrick helped him with his studies, and Eddie got such good marks that he was able to skip several grades.

The more Eddie studied the more certain he was that he wanted to be a priest. He wanted to use the fine education he was getting to help other people.

When Eddie was fourteen, his parents sent him to a boarding school in Sligo, a town on the seacoast. The school helped boys start on the long path to the priesthood.

It was a strict school. One of Eddie's friends, a boy named Mac, was full of high spirits and often got in trouble. One night Eddie dropped by Mac's room for a visit and found him packing his trunk.

"Where are you going?" Eddie asked.

"Home," Mac said. "I've been expelled from school."

"What in the world for?"

"I was caught smoking a cigarette," Mac said.

When Mac was sent home the next day, Eddie was upset. He knew it was wrong to break rules, but he believed a boy should be forgiven a mistake.

"They could have punished Mac some other way," Eddie told a classmate. "He probably won't be able to get into another school now." Eddie knew that without an education, Mac would have a hard time making a living when he grew up.

Eddie was homesick at the Sligo school, but he stayed there for four years. He enjoyed the letters from his family, especially those from Nellie and Patrick, both of whom were now living in America.

At that time Ireland was a poor country, and many people were emigrating to the United States where there was more opportunity. Nellie was working in New York City and Patrick, now a priest, was with a church in Omaha, Nebraska.

Soon after Eddie graduated from boarding school, Nellie returned to Ireland for a visit. She talked about the wonders of America all the time.

Eddie told her that he was planning to study for the priesthood in Ireland, as Patrick had done.

"Why not come to the United States?" Nellie asked. "America has excellent schools and colleges. You can study for the priesthood there."

That sounded fine to Eddie. "Why not?" he said. "I'll speak to mother and father about it."

"Good!" Nellie cried. "America needs more priests—especially Irish priests. Millions of Irishmen are living in America."

Nellie returned to New York, and Eddie followed her not long afterwards. He was six feet tall now, eighteen years old, and full of excitement at the thought of living in a new country.

When his ship arrived in New York, Nellie was on the dock, waving her handkerchief. "Welcome to America!" Nellie shouted with a smile.

2. America

Nellie told Eddie that many young men studied for the priesthood at St. Joseph's Seminary, which was at Dunwoodie, a few miles from New York City. "First, you must talk with Archbishop John Farley," Nellie said.

"I'm glad you want to be a priest," the archbishop told Eddie. "But you're still young. Do you have a college degree?"

"No, sir," Eddie admitted.

"You should get one before you go to Dunwoodie," the archbishop advised Eddie.

At the archbishop's suggestion, Eddie enrolled at Mount St. Mary's, a college

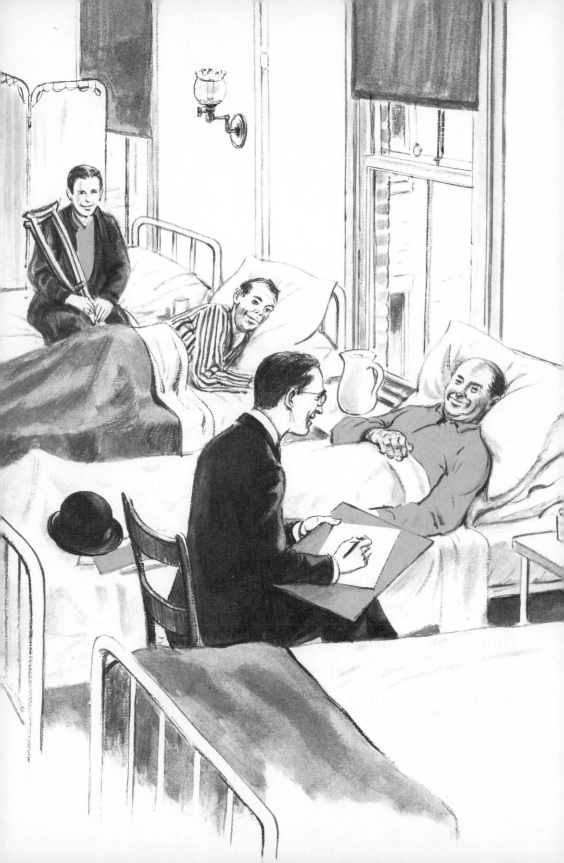

near Baltimore, Maryland. Eddie worked so hard at Mount St. Mary's that he was able to get his degree in two years. Then he went to Dunwoodie to begin his studies for the priesthood.

Though Eddie had a great deal of school-work, he volunteered to visit the sick in a New York hospital. Many of the patients had recently moved to America from Ireland, and they always cheered up when Eddie came to see them. They liked Eddie's friendly smile, and they loved to hear him tell jokes in his Irish brogue that reminded them of home. Some of the patients were so sick that they could not write letters to the families they had left behind, so Eddie wrote for them.

Shortly after Christmas during his first year at Dunwoodie, Eddie caught pneumonia. He was put to bed with a high fever in the seminary's infirmary. He lost so much weight that Nellie was shocked when she visited him. For a while his doctor was not even certain he would live.

Weeks went by, and then one day the doctor gave Eddie some great news. "You can go back to classes tomorrow," he said, "but remember you still have a cough. You must take it easy."

Eddie was behind in his class work, so he stayed up late every night trying to catch up. Examinations were coming soon, and he wanted to do well in them. Eddie made good grades, but the hard work and lack of sleep had worn him out. His cough became much worse.

Finally he went back to the infirmary. His doctor told him that he could not return to classes after vacation. "You'll kill yourself if you do," the doctor warned.

"You need lots of rest and plenty of fresh air. Try to get away from New York."

Eddie was heartbroken. His dreams of becoming a priest were shattered, at least temporarily. For the first time in his life Eddie knew the meaning of despair, but he refused to give up. "After I get well, I'm going to try again," he said.

He wrote to Patrick in Omaha and told him he was coming out for a visit. Patrick was happy to see his younger brother, but he was worried about him. "You must get well," he said.

Eddie rested, and soon the color came back to his cheeks. Finally he stopped coughing.

"Introduce me to the bishop of Omaha," Eddie said to his brother one day. "Perhaps he can help me study for the priesthood here."

Bishop Scannell of Omaha was impressed by Eddie's earnestness and friendly manner. "I believe you will make a good priest," he said. "We need more priests like your brother here in Nebraska."

"Where can I study?" Eddie asked.

"How would you like to study in Rome?"

Eddie was almost speechless. Rome was the center of the Catholic world. As far back as he could remember, Eddie had heard about the Vatican where the pope lived and the beautiful buildings there.

Finally, Eddie managed to say, "I'd rather go to Rome than anywhere else in the world."

The bishop smiled. "Your brother has told me that you made good grades at Mount St. Mary's and at St. Joseph's, and I believe you will do well in Rome. The church will pay your expenses there."

3. A Priest at Last!

Eddie arrived in Italy in the fall of 1907 and started studying at the Gregorian University in Rome. His classmates, all candidates for the priesthood, were from Africa, Asia, South America, and many other parts of the world. Eddie learned that people are pretty much the same no matter where they come from or what the color of their skin may be.

He enjoyed being in Rome. Whenever he had a spare hour, he wandered through the streets visiting the ancient buildings and monuments. However, these sightseeing trips were infrequent, for he took his studies seriously. He worked late every night and seldom got enough sleep.

When winter arrived, Eddie caught a bad cold, and before long he was coughing again. A friend told him that he must see a doctor.

"I'm afraid he'd make me leave the university," Eddie said. "Then I might never get to be a priest."

"What good is a dead priest?" his friend argued.

Reluctantly, Eddie agreed to see a doctor. The doctor was shocked when he examined him.

"Your cough is dangerous," he said, "to you and to everybody you meet. You are too thin and weak. If you stay here much longer, the damp Roman winter will either

kill you or make you an invalid for the rest of your life."

Once more Eddie had to give up his studies. He was bitterly disappointed, but he refused to abandon his ambition of becoming a priest. "I'll return to Omaha," he decided, "and rest up. Then I'll try again."

Eddie's parents and his sister Nellie, who were now living in Omaha, met him at the railroad station there. The Flanagans were distressed at the way Eddie looked, but they tried not to show it. They insisted, however, that Eddie get plenty of good food and rest.

Nobody could make Eddie stay idle for long. "I'll get a job that won't tire me out," he told Patrick. He found one as a bookkeeper, and before long he was learning a great deal about financial matters, knowledge that was to be helpful later on.

Eddie liked being busy and quickly began to gain weight. After two years in Omaha, he felt better than he had in all his life. He went to see his brother and said, "I want to try for the priesthood again."

"Fine!" Patrick said. "Let's go to see the bishop."

"I like people who won't give up," the

bishop said to Eddie. "The world needs priests like you."

A big smile spread across Eddie's face. "May I go back to..."

"Rome?" the bishop interrupted. "The climate there is bad for you."

"It certainly is," Patrick agreed. "Bishop, what do you think about the University of Innsbruck in the Austrian Alps?"

"It's a fine university," the bishop said, "and the climate is good for people with lung trouble." He turned to Eddie. "Son," he said, "I'll be happy to recommend you for the University of Innsbruck."

Eddie leaped to his feet and shook hands with the bishop. "Oh, thank you, sir!" he cried.

The University of Innsbruck accepted Eddie, and he went to Europe again. When he reached Innsbruck, he gazed in wonder

Eddie and his friends take time to enjoy the Innsbruck countryside. Eddie is third from left, without a hat.

at the lofty, snow-covered mountains that seemed to hang over the town.

Eddie was delighted with the university's fine library. However, he forced himself not to work as hard as he had at Dunwoodie and Rome. The university did not have set times for examinations, and students could take them whenever they felt they were ready.

So Eddie took his time. He knew this would probably be his last chance to become a priest, and he was determined not to get sick again.

For fun, Eddie often climbed the nearby mountains with his classmates. The exercise was good for him, and he stayed in excellent health.

In 1912, shortly after his twenty-sixth birthday, Eddie was ready to become a priest. With nine others in his class, he went to Innsbruck's St. Ignatius Church for the ceremony. In a procession led by the bishop, he walked slowly to the altar.

Two by two the candidates knelt before the bishop, who placed his hands on their heads and blessed them. When Eddie's turn came, he was filled with a great feeling of peace. The bishop drew a cross on Eddie's hands with holy oil. Later he handed him the sacred chalice, symbolizing the fact that Eddie was now eligible to celebrate mass.

At last Eddie was Father Flanagan. It was hard for him to believe it. "Father Flanagan," he whispered to himself. "I'm now Father Flanagan."

Eddie couldn't help being proud, but he was humble too. He was ready now to devote the rest of his life to God and to all mankind.

4. Homeless Men

When Father Flanagan returned to Nebraska, the bishop sent him to be the assistant priest in a small farming town. The young priest got some excellent experience looking after the spiritual needs of the people there. He celebrated mass and officiated at baptisms, weddings, and funerals. His warmth and humor made him popular with his parishioners.

After six months the bishop ordered him to return to Omaha where he became the assistant priest of a much larger church. There were many poverty-stricken men living, or trying to live, near the church. Because a drought had ruined the crops in Nebraska and neighboring states, many unemployed harvesters had come to Omaha looking for work.

Father Flanagan tried to help them find jobs, but there was almost none to be had. Most of the jobless men were soon penniless, hungry, and filled with despair. They had no place to live and had to sleep in doorways and vacant lots.

Even though he could not find jobs for the men, Father Flanagan was determined to help them. They urgently needed food and a warm place to sleep. The young priest decided to start a home for them.

He went to see some friends and told them about his plan. They were not rich, but they gave him as much money as they could to help him get started.

32

After searching for many days, he found an old building that had once been a hotel. The windows were broken, the plaster cracked, and cobwebs and dust were everywhere. There was even a hole in the roof. But if the rent were low enough, Father Flanagan thought it might be the place he was looking for.

The owner agreed to rent the hotel to Father Flanagan for a few dollars a month. "I'll fix the roof," the man said, "but you must clean up the place."

That night Father Flanagan went to a vacant lot where some of the homeless men were huddled around a fire. "I want to start a home for you men," he said. "I already have a building, but it's dirty and rundown. Will you help me fix it up?"

"We have no money for rent," one of the men said.

"The home will be free for every man who cannot find a job," Father Flanagan promised.

He persuaded hardware stores to contribute paint, plaster, window panes, and other supplies for the home. The men painted the floors, plastered the walls, and fixed the windows.

Soon after the home opened, 100 men were living there. Father Flanagan begged food from grocery stores, bakeries, and food companies. All the meals were simple, but the hungry men welcomed them. They cooked the meals, washed the dishes, and swept the floors. Rough as it was, the hotel was the best home many had ever known.

Father Flanagan still tried to find jobs for the men, and sometimes he succeeded. Those who got jobs paid for their bed and board.

When summer came, many of the men left the hotel and found work on farms. However, Father Flanagan wanted to be prepared for more homeless men the following winter. Unskilled workers lost their jobs when the ground was frozen.

Soon Father Flanagan found a bigger building and opened a new home. He called it the Workingmen's Hotel, even though most of the men who stayed there were unemployed. News of the free hotel spread throughout Nebraska and nearby states, and many jobless men came from these areas.

Some of these men were troublemakers. Others were drunkards and dope addicts, while still others had criminal records. Most of the men had never had a chance to get a decent education or learn a trade. Nobody wanted to hire them.

Naturally, these men hated themselves and one another. They got in fights and were often arrested by the police.

Father Flanagan spent many hours talking to these men, trying to persuade them to put their faith in God and to become good citizens.

"It's too late now," most of the men told him. "We're just bums."

Father Flanagan thought there must be some explanation why their lives had been ruined. He asked them many questions about their backgrounds. What were their parents like? Were the men happy when they were children? Did their mothers and fathers love them?

The young priest was struck by the fact that all the men seemed to have one thing in common—an unhappy childhood. Most of them came from broken homes. Many had never known their parents and had never been loved by anybody.

Father Flanagan could not help comparing their boyhoods with his own. He had been brought up in a loving household and had had a good education. Perhaps if these men had been happy as children, they would be good citizens now.

One night Father Flanagan was working at his desk in the hotel's lobby when he heard the door open. Looking up, he

saw a boy about nine years old standing in the doorway. The little fellow was thin and pale, and the priest could tell he was hungry. The boy's pants were torn, and his shirt was dirty. But Father Flanagan felt sure that beneath the dirty shirt there was the heart of a good boy.

"Come in, son," Father Flanagan said. "What can I do for you?"

"Are you Father Flanagan?" the boy asked.

"Yes," the priest said. "Your name is..."

"Paul. I need help."

"What's the matter?"

"I don't have any place to live," the boy said, fighting back the tears.

"Let me get you something to eat," Father Flanagan said, "and you can tell me all about it."

He took Paul into the kitchen and filled

a plate with food. The boy gobbled it down as if he had never eaten before.

Between bites he told Father Flanagan that his father had left home years before. His mother had died earlier that month, and he had been sleeping in the streets ever since. Sometimes he found a little food in garbage cans.

Father Flanagan's heart went out to the boy, and he let him stay at the hotel for several days. But he knew that Paul could not live there permanently and grow up surrounded by drunkards and criminals.

If a good home were not found for Paul, Father Flanagan knew that his life would be hopelessly ruined. Father Flanagan thought about it for a long time. "There are no bad boys," he said to himself. "Just bad parents, bad environment, and yes, bad luck."

5. Homeless Boys

Father Flanagan found a childless couple who liked Paul and was happy to adopt him. Paul was lucky, for there were many more homeless boys than there were childless couples.

Boys were homeless for various reasons. Some, of course, were orphans. Some had run away from home because their parents were cruel to them. The parents of others were so poor, or so ill, that they were unable to care for their children.

Concerned for the welfare of such boys, Father Flanagan investigated to see how they were cared for. He was shocked when he learned that many homeless boys were sent to reform schools even though they had done nothing wrong.

"There just isn't any other place to send them," a welfare officer told the priest.

Father Flanagan did not believe that any boys should be sent to reform schools. "Even if they have done something wrong, it is not their fault," he said. "The real criminals are the parents and relatives who have not brought them up properly. Perhaps all of us grownups are at fault for not helping these boys when they need help."

He learned that some boys, homeless and hungry, had been arrested and sent to reform schools for stealing apples and doughnuts. Others were guilty of more serious crimes. However, Father Flanagan believed that they could grow up to be good citizens if they were properly cared for.

"No boys get the proper care at reform schools," he told the welfare officer. "Why, reform schools are just schools for crime. They make big criminals out of little ones." He said that the younger boys were taught criminal ways by the older boys who had learned them from vicious and hardened criminals.

"There is too much harsh punishment and regimentation in the reform schools," Father Flanagan went on, "and not enough kindness and understanding. Little attention is paid to the individual child. The schools seldom succeed in reforming the boys."

"Youngsters need places where they can live normal lives," he continued. "They need love."

Later Father Flanagan heard that an Omaha judge had decided to send five homeless boys, three of whom were guilty of petty crimes, to reform school. He persuaded the judge to parole the boys in his charge.

He knew that he would have to make a home for the boys. No one wanted to adopt boys who had been sentenced to reform school. He went to a real estate agent and explained that he wanted to rent a big house.

"I think I have just the place for you," the agent said. "The rent will be only ninety dollars a month."

"Only ninety dollars!" Father Flanagan exclaimed. That was a large sum in those days. He didn't have ninety dollars.

However, he hesitated for hardly a moment. "I'll get the money if I have to..."

He stopped and started laughing. He had almost said, "if I have to steal it."

He went to see some of the people who had helped him start his hotel for homeless men and explained his plan for helping homeless boys. They gave him some money.

The house he rented was unfurnished, so Father Flanagan asked people to give him furniture they didn't need. He had become good at persuading people to contribute to worthy causes.

Just before Christmas in 1917, Father Flanagan and his five boys moved into the home. One room was made into a small chapel, and the archbishop of Omaha came to dedicate it.

"Your work is so important," the archbishop told Father Flanagan, "that I'm going to relieve you of your duties as

These boys had been sentenced to reform school, but Father Flanagan persuaded a judge to put them in his charge. With them, he moved into this house in Omaha.

assistant priest. I want you to devote all your time to helping homeless boys."

The five boys paroled in Father Flanagan's care were between eight and ten years of age. By the end of the first week, fifteen other homeless boys had moved into the house. Two nuns helped Father Flanagan look after them, and his mother and his sister often helped too.

At first there wasn't much to eat, but many people liked what Father Flanagan was doing, and they gave him all the money and food they could afford.

Someone even promised Father Flanagan that he would send a turkey with all the trimmings for the home's first Christmas dinner. The boys looked forward to a wonderful feast, but there was a mix-up and the turkey never came. Instead, a truck delivered a whole barrel of sauerkraut.

"That's all right, boys," Father Flanagan said with a grin. "It will taste just like turkey."

At dinner time all the boys sat at the long table. A big platter, piled high with sauerkraut, was set in front of Father Flanagan's place.

After he recited the blessing, Father Flanagan asked, "Who likes white meat?"

"I do," a boy halfway down the table said. Father Flanagan filled a plate with sauerkraut and passed it to the boy.

"I'd like a drumstick, Father," another boy said. When he had tasted the sauerkraut, the boy grinned and exclaimed, "Why, this is the best turkey I've ever tasted!"

After dinner the boys sang carols and played games. It was a merry Christmas after all.

Right after Christmas, when the next month's rent was almost due, Father Flanagan went to work to raise more money. He called on many businessmen, and most of them were glad to help.

Homeless boys of all religions and all races were made welcome at Father Flanagan's home. There were Catholics, Jews, and Protestants; black boys as well as white; American Indians, Mexicans, and Orientals.

Help for Father Flanagan's home came from people of all religions and all races. A Jewish man named Henry Monsky not only gave money himself, but also helped Father Flanagan raise more.

The boys at the home attended public school in Omaha. After school they did chores around the house. They swept the floors and helped prepare meals.

One night at supper, a boy turned to Father Flanagan and said, "We've got nearly everything in this house, but one thing is missing."

"What's that?" Father Flanagan asked.

"A dog," the boy said.

"Can we have a dog?" another boy asked.

"We'll take care of it," a third boy promised.

Father Flanagan had no money to buy a dog, but he found a friend whose collie had had puppies a few weeks before. The friend told him to come and get one.

Boarding a streetcar, Father Flanagan went to his friend's house, which was six miles away. He picked out a lively puppy, hid it inside his coat, and then climbed aboard a streetcar for the return trip.

Suddenly, the puppy gave a yelp. The motorman stopped the car.

CHICAGO HEIGHTS PUBLIC LIBRARY

Jb
F583g
C.1

"Father," he said, "you know dogs are not allowed on streetcars."

"This is just a puppy," Father Flanagan said.

"A rule is a rule," the motorman insisted. "You'll have to get off here."

The night was cold and windy, but Father Flanagan walked the six miles home, carrying the puppy inside his coat. The boys were waiting for him. They were delighted with their pet, and they named him Carlo.

6. "He Ain't Heavy, Father..."

The population of Father Flanagan's home grew rapidly, and soon he needed a larger house. He found one with a big field behind it where the boys could play football, baseball, and basketball.

One day a truck stopped in front of the new home. A farmer got out and asked to see Father Flanagan. "I'd like to give you some money," the farmer said, "but I don't have any extra cash. So I want your boys to have the cow I've got in my truck."

The boys took turns milking the cow. They raised chickens too and planted a garden. Father Flanagan was glad they were learning how to work and to accept responsibility. He felt sure they would grow up to be good citizens.

Not everybody agreed with him, however. Many of the other children at the public schools called Father Flanagan's boys "gangsters" and refused to play with them.

Actually, only a small percentage of the boys had criminal records, and they were becoming happy, law-abiding youngsters under Father Flanagan's care. All they needed, he felt, was moral training, someone truly interested in them, and the family atmosphere the home provided.

Yet even some of the public school officials complained about Father Flanagan's boys. "They belong in reform schools," one man told Father Flanagan.

Angered by the prejudice against his boys, Father Flanagan started a school at his home. At first the faculty consisted of the two nuns, Father Flanagan, and his nephew Patrick Norton, who had recently come from Ireland to help run the home for boys.

News of the work Father Flanagan was doing spread throughout the United States. Homeless boys from many parts of the country hitchhiked, or rode on freight trains, to Omaha. Others were brought by their widowed or divorced mothers who had no money to care for their sons.

Father Flanagan took as many of these boys as he could, but of course he could not take them all. There just wasn't room —or enough money.

He was sorry that he had to turn some boys away. However, even if he had enough money, he felt he could never accept boys who were badly handicapped. They needed special facilities and special help that were not available at the home.

One night Father Flanagan was told that a woman and her son were in his office, waiting to see him. When Father Flanagan reached his office he saw a tired, shabbily dressed woman and a pale eight-year-old boy.

"I'm Father Flanagan," he said, shaking hands with them. The woman stood up, but the boy remained seated.

"I can't take care of my son," the woman said. "His father deserted us and I have to work all day. There is no one to look after him." The woman started crying.

Father Flanagan really didn't have room just then for even one extra boy, but he felt sorry for the poor woman. "We're crowded," he began, "and..."

"Please, Father," the woman sobbed.

He patted the woman on the shoulder, trying to comfort her. "We'll find room for your son," he said.

"Oh, thank you, Father!" the woman cried. She kissed her son and quickly left the office. Father Flanagan turned to the boy and said, "I'll take you to your room. Come with me."

"I can't walk, Father," the boy said slowly. "I—I'm crippled."

Father Flanagan made up his mind immediately to break his rule and let the boy stay at the home. He'd find some way to help him. "That's all right, son," he said. "I'll get someone to carry you."

He sent for an older boy named Joe. When Joe arrived at the office, Father Flanagan lifted the crippled boy in his arms and put him gently on Joe's back.

As he did so, he asked, "Is he too heavy, Joe?"

"He ain't heavy, Father," Joe said. "He's m' brother."

Father Flanagan smiled. "That's not the best grammar, Joe, but it's a fine idea. 'He ain't heavy, he's m' brother.' I think that should be our home's motto."

Joe carried the crippled boy to his room. Later Father Flanagan got expert medical care for him, and the boy learned to walk with a cane. He was even able to help do some of the work around the home.

There was soon plenty of work for everyone. Father Flanagan bought 40 acres of land on the outskirts of Omaha, and the boys started farming on a big scale.

As he now had more than 100 boys to care for, Father Flanagan wanted to build a large house on the farm and move out there. Some people who lived near the farm became angry when they heard about Father Flanagan's plans.

"Many of your boys are criminals," they said. "We don't want them for neighbors."

"My boys are just as good as any boys in Nebraska," Father Flanagan retorted, "probably better than most."

Still he did not want his boys to grow up in a place where they were not welcome. Many had come to him originally because they were not wanted even by their parents. Instead of hatred and contempt, they needed friendship and love.

So Father Flanagan sold the 40 acres. With the money he received and with gift

60

Father Flanagan leads the boys in a gala
parade in the 1920s.

money from many people, he bought a
much bigger farm about eleven miles
from Omaha where there were no close
neighbors. His good friend Henry Monsky
helped raise over $200,000 to build dormi-
tories, dining halls, classrooms, athletic
fields, and a chapel.

In 1921, only four years after Father
Flanagan started helping homeless boys,

he and his charges moved to their new home. At first, it was called Overlook Farm, but later the official name became Father Flanagan's Boys' Home.

Besides raising crops and livestock, the boys took care of the grounds, mended shoes, washed clothes, and even printed a newspaper. Some boys learned to be mechanics; others learned to bake bread and cut hair. Father Flanagan wanted every boy to learn a trade so that he could support himself when he was old enough to leave the home.

Most boys stayed at the home until they had finished high school. Some got scholarships and went on to college, but most went right to work and became respected members of their communities.

7. The Barefoot Slayer

In 1931 Father Flanagan's Boys' Home was almost fifteen years old. During those years Father Flanagan had worked hard raising money for the home, planning new buildings, and caring for his boys.

Some of his friends felt that he was working too hard, and they wanted him to take a long vacation.

"My job is here," Father Flanagan said, and he went on as before.

One morning he started to cough. His cough rapidly became worse, and he started losing weight.

"You must go to a hospital and take a complete rest," his doctor said. "Otherwise you won't be able to work here or anywhere else. You are only 45 years old. You'll have many good years ahead if you take care of yourself."

Father Flanagan went to a hospital, and after resting a few weeks, he began to feel better. The better he felt the more restless he became.

One day he read in a newspaper that a twelve-year-old boy named Herbert had been sentenced to life imprisonment for murder. He was horrified and discussed the case with his nurse.

"No boy of twelve can be a murderer at heart," he said.

"Herbert admits he killed a sheriff," the nurse reminded him.

"I still say there are no bad boys,"

Father Flanagan argued. "There are just bad parents and bad examples. I'm sure poor Herbert never had a chance. I'd like to give him one."

In the newspapers Father Flanagan read that Herbert had tried to rob a store late one night in a little town in the state of Washington. The sheriff had heard a noise coming from inside the store and had gone with his assistant to investigate.

When they entered the store Herbert, who had a loaded gun, hid behind a pickle barrel. As the sheriff leaned over the barrel, Herbert jumped up and fired his gun. The sheriff fell dead at his feet.

The sheriff's assistant caught Herbert, and the boy was brought to trial. The jury found him guilty of murder, and the judge sentenced him to life imprisonment in the state penitentiary.

Poor Herbert's fate weighed on Father Flanagan's conscience.

"I must go to see the governor of Washington," he said. "I'd like to have that boy in my home."

"You should stay in bed," his nurse said.

"I'm all right now," Father Flanagan argued. "I must try to help Herbert."

When he got to Washington, Father Flanagan learned that Herbert had had a most unhappy childhood. His father was mentally ill and had been in a hospital for many years. His mother had not been able to take care of him properly. The boy was allowed to roam the streets every night. He rarely had enough to eat or enough clothes. Because he wore no shoes when he committed the murder, the newspapers called him the "barefoot slayer."

When he was only nine, Herbert had

stolen an automobile. Later, when desperate for food, he had robbed a post office and was sent to a reform school.

"Reform schools are just crime factories," Father Flanagan grunted when he heard about it. He admitted, however, that even a reform school would be a better place for Herbert than a penitentiary.

He went to talk with the governor of Washington and asked him to parole Herbert in his care.

"Herbert is a murderer," the governor insisted.

"I've helped young criminals before. I know I can turn this boy into a useful citizen," Father Flanagan said.

The governor agreed to think over Father Flanagan's proposal, but he promised nothing.

After Father Flanagan left, the governor announced that Herbert must go to prison for life. He said that Father Flanagan was just trying to get publicity for his home.

Father Flanagan was sick at heart when he learned that his efforts to save Herbert had been in vain. He was also furious with the governor. "Father Flanagan's Boys' Home does not need publicity," he told reporters. "One of the boys at my home was a killer at nine," he said. "Now he is a model boy. Herbert would be too if he were given a chance."

Though Father Flanagan was unable to save Herbert from prison, some good did come of his efforts. Eventually a law was passed in the state of Washington that all child criminals must be sent to training schools and not to penitentiaries. That pleased Father Flanagan.

He was also pleased when he learned that Herbert, after serving ten years, was finally paroled at the age of twenty-two. Perhaps he could still lead a useful life.

8. Happy Ending to a Sad Story

Sometimes people wanted to adopt boys from Father Flanagan's home. At first he approved. He felt that boys would be happier if they were members of real families.

However, not all the people who said they wanted to adopt boys were honest. Many farmers often came to see Father Flanagan in the spring saying that they would like to adopt a boy on a trial basis. After six months they would decide if they wanted the boy permanently.

The story was nearly always the same. A farmer would pick out a strong, healthy boy and leave with him. At the farm the boy would work all day long, plowing, planting, and hoeing. He would feed the chickens and livestock, chop wood, and harvest the crops.

Usually the boy was willing to work hard, for he wanted to please the farmer and be adopted. At the end of the trial period, however, late in the fall when most of the farm work was done, the farmer would bring the boy back to the home.

"This boy is no good, Father," the farmer would say. "I don't want him."

Father Flanagan finally caught on. The farmers just wanted free labor on their farms during the growing season. They had no intention of adopting the boys permanently.

After that experience Father Flanagan was wary about letting his boys be adopted. However, he was still glad to send them to happy homes.

One day he received a telegram from a wealthy man who wanted to adopt a boy named Pete. The man and his wife had seen Pete's picture in the home's newspaper, which was sent all over America. They thought Pete looked exactly like their only son who had recently drowned.

In the telegram the man said that he and his wife wanted Pete to take the place of their lost son. They would send him to college and later give him a fine job in their business.

They suggested that Pete live with them for three months. Then, if they got along with each other, the couple would adopt Pete legally.

As soon as he finished reading the telegram, Father Flanagan sent for Pete and asked him what he thought of the idea.

"It sounds great!" Pete cried.

"You must realize," Father Flanagan said, "that this may not work out. I'm afraid the man wants you to act, as well as look, like his dead son."

"I'd like to try it," Pete said. "It's a chance for me to get a college education. And I'd like to have a family of my own."

Father Flanagan arranged for Pete to spend the summer with the people who had lost their son.

"It seems like a dream," Pete told Father Flanagan when he said good-bye. "I'm afraid I'll wake up."

Stories about Pete and the family appeared in many newspapers. When Pete

arrived at his new home, he was surrounded by reporters and photographers.

"I'll have to get used to sleeping in a
room by myself," Pete told his new father
and mother while the reporters listened.
"At the home I had 30 roommates."

At first Pete got along well with his
new parents. On his fourteenth birthday,
they had a party for him and gave him a
bicycle and some new clothes. Pete liked
to wear overalls as he often did in Nebraska, but his new parents would not
allow that. They made him wear fancy
shorts.

In letters to Father Flanagan, Pete said
he was getting along fine. Later on, however, while Father Flanagan was on a trip
abroad, he was distressed to learn that
Pete was back at the home. The boy's
would-be father had said that Pete was

disobedient and very arrogant. "Too much publicity turned the boy's head," he said.

When Father Flanagan returned from his trip, he tried to see the man and his wife. They refused to talk to him.

As soon as he reached the home, he sent for Pete. "I'm sorry, son," he said.

"I don't think I was disobedient or arrogant," Pete said. "I didn't intend to be."

"I know you were not, Pete," Father Flanagan said. "That man wanted you to be like his dead son, but nobody can be like someone else."

With tears in his eyes, Pete said, "I did the best I could. I tried to be what they wanted me to be, but I guess I just couldn't do that. I had never been used to a family. Maybe I just didn't know how to act."

"Cheer up, Pete," Father Flanagan said. "Maybe it really is true that everything happens for the best."

A short time later Father Flanagan sent for Pete again. As Pete walked into the office, he saw a tall young man standing by Father Flanagan's desk. He was a stranger, but he didn't look like a stranger —he looked like Pete.

Pete was astonished. Could this be the boy who was supposedly drowned? Was there some ghastly mistake?

Father Flanagan saw the puzzled look on Pete's face. "Pete," he said, "shake hands with your brother."

"My brother!" Pete exclaimed. "I haven't got a brother!"

"Sit down, Pete," Father Flanagan said, "and I'll try to explain. You have two older brothers and one older sister. When you were a baby, all four of you were sent to different orphans' homes."

"I'm your brother Chris," the older boy said. "We didn't know where you were until we saw your picture and name in the newspapers. We didn't want to get in touch with you at first as we hoped you'd be happy with your new family. But we're glad it didn't work out. We want you to come and live with us."

So Pete was adopted again—by his own brothers and sister. This time he did not come back to the home.

9. Boys Town, U.S.A.

As years went by, Father Flanagan's Boys' Home grew until it was larger than many small towns. In the early 1930s, the home had a swimming pool, a theater, an infirmary, and a gymnasium. There were also a bakery, a barber shop, a laundry, and a power plant.

Even though there were several hundred boys in the home now, Father Flanagan knew them all by their first names. The boys always enjoyed visiting his office, for he took such a warm interest in their problems. There were fatherlike counselors in each dormitory, and new, familylike cottages were being planned.

Father Flanagan himself lived in a cottage with his sister Nellie, who had been working with him for many years. Laymen as well as priests were on the teaching staff.

"We're not just a home anymore," Father Flanagan told Nellie one day. "We're a real town—a boys town."

Ever since the move to the farm, people had nicknamed the home "Boys Town." Now, at Father Flanagan's suggestion, the state of Nebraska made "Boys Town" officially a village, and the United States government set up a post office called Boys Town, Nebraska. Soon the name appeared on maps.

One day Father Flanagan called a meeting of all his boys. "We're a real town

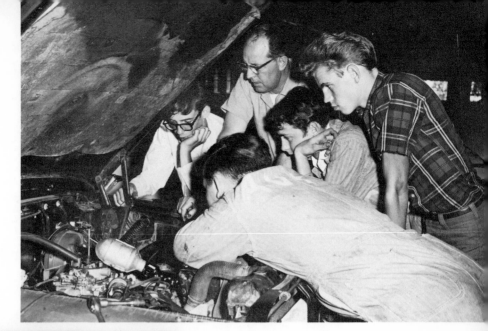

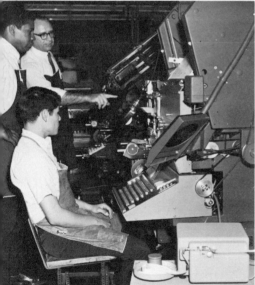

Father Flanagan wanted his boys to learn skills
so that they could find good jobs when they left
Boys Town. Among trades taught there today are
auto repairing, linotype operating, and baking.

now," he said, "but there's one thing every town needs that we don't have."

"What's that, Father?" a boy asked.

"We don't have a town government. It's time we have one. You boys are going to run it."

Father Flanagan explained that the boys should elect a mayor, who would serve for six months. They would also elect commissioners, who would work with the mayor. There would be a police department and a fire department.

"This is going to be the only town in the world," Father Flanagan said with a grin, "where all the voters are under twenty-one."

The boys were enthusiastic about the idea. They formed political parties, made up campaign slogans, and elected a mayor.

The mayor and the commissioners made

some laws. Clothes had to be hung up, sporting equipment returned to its proper place, and each boy had to make his own bed.

"When boys break the laws," Father Flanagan told the mayor and the commissioners, "you municipal officials have to punish them. You know I always say there's no such thing as a bad boy. But there certainly are some ornery ones."

The officials thought up some clever ways to punish the offenders. Sometimes boys who broke the laws were denied use of the swimming pool. But that wasn't all. They were made to undress, take a shower, put on their swimming trunks, and then stand beside the pool while the other boys swam.

Withdrawal of movie privileges was the worst punishment of all—capital punishment, the boys called it. Movies were shown at Boys Town once a week. If a boy had been unusually bad, he was made to come to the movie and stand with his back toward the screen. He could hear the sound, but couldn't see a thing.

"That's cruel," Father Flanagan said, trying not to laugh, when the mayor told him about capital punishment.

"Sorry if it distresses you, Father," the mayor declared, "but it works. We rarely have to punish the same boy twice."

Father Flanagan was pleased with the way the boys ran their town. Once he took the mayor, a boy named Daniel Kampan, on a trip to New York City. Father Flanagan made speeches there to raise money for Boys Town.

While in New York he and Daniel were invited to meet Mayor Fiorello La Guardia at City Hall. Father Flanagan let the two mayors confer. The mayors of America's largest city and one of its smallest decided they had many similar problems.

"Being mayor isn't what it's cracked up to be," Mayor La Guardia said. "It's a lot of hard work." The mayor of Boys Town agreed with him.

Newspaper photographers wanted to take a picture of Father Flanagan and the two mayors, but Father Flanagan refused to be in the photograph. "This is a meeting of two famous mayors," he said. "I'd be out of place."

Shortly afterwards two movies were made about Boys Town. Millions of people saw the movies, and Father Flanagan became famous.

People were impressed by the way he treated homeless boys. They began to

agree with him that love, not punishment, should be used to help boys grow up to be good citizens.

Father Flanagan believed that sports were also important. "If a boy learns to play a game hard and fair," he said, "the chances are that he will play life that way too."

Boys Town teams played many high schools in the area and usually won. Father Flanagan wanted his boys to win, but he also wanted them to be good sports.

One day the Boys Town varsity basketball team was playing an important game. At half time the rival team was ahead.

The Boys Town captain turned to Father Flanagan and said, "No wonder they're winning. They're hitting us with elbows, knees, everything!"

"So what?" Father Flanagan shot back.

"They're cheating, that's what!" the boy said. "It's not fair. Why can't we use our knees and elbows too? Maybe we could win."

"Do you want to win that way?" Father Flanagan asked.

The boy looked down at his feet. He was ashamed of himself. "No, Father," he said. "I don't really want to win that way."

In the second half the Boys Town team fought a hard, clean game. In the last few minutes they pulled ahead, and when the final whistle blew, Boys Town had won. Father Flanagan cheered loudly. He was proud that his boys were both good basketball players and good sports.

10. Father Flanagan's Work Goes On

When America entered World War II in 1941, many of Father Flanagan's older boys wanted to enlist at once. He persuaded them to wait until they had finished high school.

He hated war, but he was proud of the record Boys Town graduates made. Seven hundred and fifty served honorably in the armed forces, and many were decorated for bravery.

Once during the war Father Flanagan said, "We live in peace and harmony at Boys Town. There's no reason why all of us cannot live in peace and harmony everywhere."

Father Flanagan hated racial and religious prejudice as well as war. He was pleased when his friend Henry Monsky, the lawyer who had done so much for Boys Town, became national president of B'nai B'rith. That organization not only does charitable work, but also fights religious and racial discrimination.

At a dinner in Monsky's honor, Father Flanagan was the main speaker. "Racial and religious prejudice is one of the greatest ills in American life," he said. "Americans should respect the rights of all citizens."

During World War II millions of parents were killed, leaving millions of children homeless throughout the world. Soon after the war ended, Father Flanagan went to Japan to see how the orphans were treated there. He found that many of the orphan homes were like prisons. The children worked long hours and were not allowed to go to school or to enjoy sports.

On Father Flanagan's recommendation, many changes were made, and the orphans of Japan were given a chance to grow up in a more normal way.

Millions of European children were homeless too. President Harry S. Truman asked Father Flanagan to go there and report on conditions.

Father Flanagan traveled throughout western Europe, attending meetings and discussing what should be done for the homeless children. He helped some countries set up homes modeled on Boys Town. Some were even called "Boys Town," which pleased Father Flanagan.

After World War II, Father Flanagan traveled all over the globe helping to organize homes for orphaned children. He is shown here in northern Ireland.

While in Berlin one day he went to visit a boys' home in the center of the city. He had to climb a steep flight of stairs, and when he reached the top, he felt weak and out of breath.

"I can't rest now," he said to himself. "The boys are expecting me."

That evening Father Flanagan was exhausted. He went to bed early, but in the middle of the night, he woke up with a severe pain in his chest. It was a heart attack. A few hours later Edward Joseph Flanagan was dead at the age of 61.

Father Flanagan's body was flown to Nebraska. Thousands of people, many of them former residents of Boys Town, came to his funeral. Thanks to Father Flanagan, these once homeless boys were now useful citizens with happy homes of their own.

They wept during the funeral service when they heard the words from Matthew 25:35 in the New Testament:

> For I was hungry,
>   and you gave me to eat;
> I was thirsty,
>   and you gave me to drink;
> I was a stranger,
>   and you took me in,
> ... sick, and you visited me;
> I was in prison,
>   and you came to me ...

Though Father Flanagan is dead, the work that he started goes on. Boys Town is a much larger community today than it was when he was alive. And Father Flanagan's great idea that "there is no such thing as a bad boy" has spread throughout the world.

94

CHICAGO HEIGHTS PUBLIC LIBRARY

Index

Ballymoe, 11
Berlin, 93
B'nai B'rith, 90
Boys Town, 80, 81 (pics), 82-85, 87-89, 90-91, 93-94. *See also* Father Flanagan's Boys' Home; Overlook Farm

Dunwoodie. *See* St. Joseph's Seminary

Europe, 27, 91

Farley, John, 17
Father Flanagan's Boys' Home, 62, 63, 68, 70, 79. *See also* Boys Town; Overlook Farm
Featherstone, Father, 11-12
Flanagan, Edward Joseph
    and adoption of boys, 70-75, 77-78
    boyhood of, 7, 9-16, 28 (pic), 38
    and Boys Town, 80, 82-85, 87-91, 93-94
    death of, 93-94
    education of, 13-15, 17, 19, 22-24, 26-27, 29-30
    health of, 19-21, 24-26, 63-64

and homeless boys, 39-40, 41-45, 46 (pic), 47-50, 53-57, 59-60, 61 (pic), 62-63, 70-75, 79-80, 85, 87
and jobless men, 32-34, 36-38
as priest, 30-31, 45, 47
and Workingmen's Hotel, 36, 38
and war orphans, 89-90, 92 (pic)
and young criminals, 42-43, 64-69
Flanagan, Honora (mother), 9, 10, 11, 12, 25-26, 47
Flanagan, John (father), 7, 9, 11, 25-26
Flanagan, Nellie (sister), 10, 15-17, 20, 25, 47, 80
Flanagan, Patrick (brother), 10, 12, 13, 15, 21, 26

Gregorian University, 23

Innsbruck, University of, 27
Ireland, 7, 15, 19, 55
Italy, 23

Japan, 91

Kampan, Daniel, 84-85

LaGuardia, Fiorello, 84-85

Monsky, Henry, 49, 61, 90
Mount St. Mary's College, 17, 19, 22

Nebraska, 22, 31-32, 36, 60, 80, 93
New Testament, 94
New York, 15-17, 19, 21, 84
Norton, Patrick, 55

Omaha, 15, 21, 25-26, 31-32, 44, 49, 55, 59, 61
Overlook Farm, 62. *See also* Boys Town; Father Flanagan's Boys' Home

Reform schools, 42-44, 67
Rome, 22-24, 29

St. Ignatius Church, 30
St. Joseph's Seminary, 17, 19, 22, 29
Scannell, Bishop, 22, 26-27
Sligo, 13-14

Truman, Harry S., 91

Vatican, 22

Washington, 65-67, 69
Workingmen's Hotel, 36
World War II, 89-90